You Begins Now

Pastor Robert J. Mullen

Your New Life

Unless otherwise indicated, all Scripture quotations are from the *Holy Bible, King James Version.*

Scripture quotations marked (NKJV) are from the *New King James Version.*

Scripture quotations marked (NASB) are from the *New American Standard Bible.*

Scripture quotations marked (NLT) are from the *New Living Translation.*

Scripture quotations marked (AMP) are from the *Amplified Bible.*

Scripture quotations marked (NIV) are from the *New International Version*

All rights reserved under International Copyright law. Contents and/or cover may not be reproduced in whole or in part in any form without the express written consent of the author.

Your New Life: Begins Now

ISBN   978-1-60458-415-8

Copyright © 2008 by Robert J. Mullen Ministries

PO Box 55172

Stockton, CA 95205

209-401-5591

wotwfm@aol.com

Table of Contents

Dedication 4

Foreword ……………………………………………….5

Introduction …………………………………………….6

Chapter 1: God Is Love………………………………….8
Chapter 2: Our Sin Keeps Us From God ………………12
Chapter 3: Jesus Died For Our Sins ……………………15
Chapter 4: You Must Be Born Again…………………..18
Chapter 5: Understanding Faith……………………….. 30
Chapter 6: Healing Is Yours……………………………38
Chapter 7: Baptism in the Holy Spirit………………....46
Chapter 8: The Abundant Life………………………….61

Author's Biography……………………………………71

Dedication

There are many whom I am thankful for. First and foremost, I am thankful to God and His Son Jesus Christ for delivering and saving me. I am grateful for His call on my life and the responsibility that He has entrusted me with.

I want to say thank you to my partner in ministry, my wife Tabatha, for over 20 years who has been my major support in all that I have sought out to do. She has always been by my side no matter how hard things were; I love her so very much.

I also am grateful to all of my children, Charity, Amanda, Alyssa, Ricky, and Caleb who have been through it all, and served within the ministry and in life with me. I love them so very much.

Foreword

I am excited that you have chosen to be a part of the Kingdom of God. I want to welcome you, and pray the Word of God presented in this book becomes a testimony you can share with friends and family.

Do you realize how vital it is to be taught the Word of God in a practical manner? Through this, you not only gain understanding, but you can apply it to your daily life. It's almost as important as breathing because it affects your ability to succeed.

I have committed myself to ensuring that your soul is renewed, and your spirit is revitalized and filled with God's Word. I appreciate the opportunity to minister a timely Word that gives you the answers you've been searching for.

Blessings,

Pastor Robert J. Mullen

Introduction

Welcome to Your New Life

There are two roads that we can travel while here on earth. The Word of God tells us in ***Matthew 7:13-14 NLT, You can enter God's Kingdom only through the narrow gate. The highway to hell is broad, and its gate is wide for the many who choose that way. But the gateway to life is very narrow and the road is difficult, and only a few ever find it.***

Therefore, we can see one gate leads to eternal life, which is where we will enjoy an unending life filled with God's light, life, joy, total health, abundance, and love. This gate is called narrow. However, this does not mean that it is difficult to become a Christian, but that there is only one way to eternal life with God the Father.

John 14:6 NLT, Jesus told him, "I am the way, the truth, and the life. No one can come to the Father except through me."

The difficulty is that only a few decide to walk that road deciding to accept God's way. The other road is broad with a wide gate that leads to a place of darkness, sin, shame, sickness, hate, and unforgiveness. Everyone is presented with a choice.

However, if you have chosen to make Jesus Christ your Lord and Savior, I want to say, *"Congratulations!"* God is your Father, Jesus is your Savior, and you are a citizen into the Kingdom of God.

In this book, you will find answers to questions that you have concerning Your New Life. You will learn what the Bible says about Sin, God's Love, Salvation, and many more things. The other purpose for this book is to give you the tools you need to share with others what the New Life is all about.

Your New Life

Chapter 1

God Is Love

How Do We Define *Love?*

"God is Love," but how do we define it? *The American Heritage Dictionary* defines love as "an intense affection for another person based on familiar or personal ties." We love other people, or we say we love other people, when we are attracted to them and when they make us feel good. Notice that a key phrase in the dictionary definition of love is the phrase "based on." This phrase implies that we love conditionally; in other words, we love someone because he or she fulfills a condition that we require before we can love him or her. How many times have you heard or said, "I love you because you are nice," or "I love you because you take good care of me," or "I love you because you are fun to be with?"

Our love is not only conditional; it is also limited. We love based on feelings and emotions that can change from one moment to the next. Marriages are often dissolved because couples say that they have fallen out of love and no longer love one another. What happens? Because they are dealing with some difficulties in their relationship and become frustrated with each other, they conclude that it is hopeless, so they give up on it and get divorced? Evidently, their marriage vow of "'Til death do us part" means they can part at the death of their love for their spouse rather than at their physical death. Can anyone really comprehend "unconditional" love? It seems the love that parents have for their children is as close to unconditional love as we can get without the help of God's love in our lives. We continue to love our children through good times and bad, and we don't stop loving them if they don't meet the expectations we may have for them. We make a choice to love our children even when we consider them unlovable; our love doesn't stop when we don't "feel" love for them. This is similar to God's love for us, but as we shall see, God's love goes beyond the human definition and understanding of love to a point that is hard for us to comprehend.

How Does *God* Define Love?

The Bible tells us that in ***I John 4:8 AMP, He who does not love has not become acquainted with God [does not and never did know Him], for God is love.*** However, how can we even begin to understand that truth? Many passages in the Bible give us God's definition of love. The most well known verse is ***John 3:16, "For God so loved the world that He gave His only begotten Son, that whoever believes in Him should not perish but have everlasting life."*** So one way God defines love is in the act of giving. However, what God gave (or should we say, "who" God gave), was not a mere gift-wrapped present; God sacrificed His only Son so that we, who put our faith in His Son, will not spend eternity separated from Him. This is an amazing love because we are the ones who choose to be separated from God through our own sin, yet it's God who mends the separation through His intense personal sacrifice, and all we have to do is accept His gift.

Another great verse about God's love is found in ***Romans 5:8, But God demonstrates His own love toward us, in that while we were still sinners, Christ died for us.*** In this verse and in *John 3:16*, we find no conditions placed on

God's love for us. God doesn't say, "As soon as you clean up your act, I'll love you;" nor does He say, "I'll sacrifice My Son if you promise to love Me." In fact, in ***Romans 5:8,*** we find just the opposite. God wants us to know that His love is unconditional, so He sent His Son, Jesus Christ, to die for us while we were still unlovable sinners. We didn't have to get clean, and we didn't have to make any promises to God before we could experience His love. His love for us has always existed, and because of that, He did all the giving and sacrificing long before we were even aware that we needed His love.

God's Love Is Unconditional

God is Love, and His love is very different from human love. God's love is unconditional, and it's not based on feelings or emotions. He doesn't love us because we're lovable or because we make Him feel good; He loves us because He is love. He created us to have a loving relationship with Him, and He sacrificed His own Son (who also willingly died for us) to restore that relationship.

Your New Life

Chapter 2

Our Sin Keeps Us From God

The fact is we need Jesus. The Bible tells us, *"For all have sinned and fall short of the glory of God." (Romans 3:23)* Though God intended for us to have a relationship with Him, we naturally want to do things our own way. We're stubborn, selfish, and frequently unable to follow through on our promises.

Deep down, our attitude may be willingly demonstrating rebellion or passive indifference, but it's all evidence of what the Bible calls sin, which literally means "missing the mark."

The Bible says the result of sin in our lives is death– spiritual separation from God.

For the wages of sin **is** *death, but the gift of God* **is** *eternal life in Jesus Christ our Lord.* **(Romans 6:23)**

Although we may try to reach God through our own effort, we will continually fail. Our own effort will never bring us to a place of being good enough.

Jesus Christ is the only One who can take care of our sins. Through Him, we can know and experience God's love and plan for our lives.

Jesus Christ is God's solution to the problem of human imperfection and evil. Because of Jesus' death on the cross, we don't have to be separated from God any longer. Jesus paid the price for our sin and in doing so, bridged the gap between God and us.

Instead of trying harder to reach God, we simply need to accept Jesus and His sacrifice as the one way to God. *Jesus said to him, "I am the way, the truth, and the life. No one comes to the Father except through Me." (John 14:6)* He also said, *"I am the resurrection and the life. Anyone who believes in me will live, even after dying. Everyone who lives in me and believes in me will never ever die. (John 11:25-26 NLT)*

Not only did Jesus die for our sin, He rose from the dead. *I passed on to you what was most important and what had also been passed on to me. Christ died for our sins, just as the Scriptures said. He was buried, and he was raised from the dead on the third day, just as the Scriptures said. He was seen by Peter and then by the Twelve. After that, he was seen by more than 500 of his followers at one time, most of whom are still alive, though some have died. (I Corinthians 15:3-6 NLT)* When He did, He proved beyond doubt that He can rightfully promise eternal life – that He is the son of God and the only means by which we can know God.

Just having knowledge about God's plans and purposes isn't enough. We need to consciously accept Jesus Christ as the payment for our sin and welcome Him into our life.

Chapter 3

Jesus Died For Our Sins

But if we are living in the light, as God is in the light, then we have fellowship with each other, and the blood of Jesus, his Son, cleanses us from all sin. (I John 1:7 NLT)

Christ's payment for our sins is so complete and sufficient that we can add nothing to it. We cannot save ourselves and we need not try because He has already paid for our sins. That is why the apostle Paul said, **"God saved you by his grace when you believed. And you can't take credit for this; it is a gift from God. Salvation is not a reward for the good things we have done, so none of us can boast about it." *(Ephesians 2:8-9 NLT)*** Salvation is a free gift of God made possible by His grace to undeserving sinners. It is not a reward for our good deeds nor is it something we must spend a lifetime trying to earn. It is a gift that we must receive by simple faith.

We need to receive salvation by faith. Knowing that Christ died in our place and that God is willing to pardon our sins will not save us until we receive that pardon by faith. If a prisoner was condemned to die and was given a pardon, he would have to receive it in order to be set free. Saving faith is simply receiving God's pardon for sin. That pardon was secured by Christ's death on the cross.

Faith is the placing of one's trust in someone or something. It means believing in someone you cannot see, but simply accepting it for what it is. For example, we are told that we have a brain and we accept that even though we have not seen it for ourselves. It means believing the word or promise of someone when he gives it to you. Saving faith is to believe in the promise of God. It is accepting the offer of salvation as a free gift from God to you personally.

Jesus said in a conversation with a man by the name of Nicodemus these things: *"I tell you the truth, unless you are born again, you cannot see the Kingdom of God." (John 3:3 NLT)* This is known as the New Birth, which is not just a nice idea, it is an encounter that we have with God. This is where we must trust the Bible and accept this experience when one is born again when he receives Jesus Christ as his personal Savior. Spiritual rebirth occurs when God is born in us and unites His Spirit with our spirit.

In the last night of His earthly ministry, Jesus prayed for all who would come to believe in Him. Jesus prayed this prayer, *"I pray that they will all be one, just as you and I are one – as you are in me, Father, and I am in you. And may they be in us so that the world will believe you sent me." (John 17:21 NLT)* Our union with Christ is to be demonstrated by our unity with other believers. The New Birth makes us children of God and adds us to the family of God. By the New Birth, we actually receive the divine nature of God Himself.

The Bible says, *If you confess with your mouth that Jesus is Lord and believe in your heart that God raised him from the dead, you will be saved. (Romans 10:9 NLT)*

We need to call upon God to save us. The invitation given to all is clear. *For "Everyone who calls on the name of the Lord will be saved." (Romans 10:13 NLT)*

In the next chapter, we will see that YOU MUST BE BORN AGAIN!

Your New Life

Chapter 4

You Must Be Born Again

Let us begin with this story in the Word of God where Jesus came to a man by the name of Nicodemus who came to Jesus one night to receive an understanding to what He was teaching. Nicodemus was a Pharisee and a ruler of the Jews. He was well educated in what the Jewish religion taught. The teaching he received does include believing in God, praying, fasting, and paying vows (tithing), attending church (known as synagogues), Scripture reading, and living according to all moral laws. Even with all of these things, Jesus told him he had to be born again in order to enter the Kingdom of God. Let us look at the conversation between Nicodemus and Jesus.

There was a man named Nicodemus, a Jewish religious leader who was a Pharisee. After dark one evening, he came to speak with Jesus. "Rabbi," he said, "we all know that God has sent you to teach us. Your miraculous signs are evidence that God is with you."

Jesus replied, "I tell you the truth, unless you are born again, you cannot see the Kingdom of God."

"What do you mean?" exclaimed Nicodemus. "How can an old man go back into his mother's womb and be born again?"

Jesus replied, "I assure you, no one can enter the Kingdom of God without being born of water and the Spirit. Humans can reproduce only human life, but the Holy Spirit gives birth to spiritual life. So don't be surprised when I say, 'You must be born again.' The wind blows wherever it wants. Just as you can hear the wind but can't tell where it comes from or where it is going, so you can't explain how people are born of the Spirit." (John 3:1-8 NLT)

The Kingdom of God in the above verse means "The Way of God" meaning God's way of doing things. In this case, it means how to be born again the way God planned for it to be. We also see in Verse 3 where it mentions *being born of water and of the Spirit.* This could mean Water baptism and a spiritual birth. Water baptism is an important part of a born again experience and is something we should do.

Later in this chapter, we will further discuss Water baptism and why it is an important part to our New Life.

According to Paul, he taught in Romans the importance of believing and confession with your mouth leading to salvation. The word *"believe"* can be defined as *trusts in, clings to,* and *relies on.* The word *confess* can be defined as *declaring openly* and *to speak out freely about one's faith.*

Salvation that comes from trusting Christ - which is the message we preach – is already within easy reach. In fact, the Scriptures say, "The message is very close at hand; it is on your lips and in your heart."

If you confess with your mouth that Jesus is Lord and believe in your heart that God raised him from the dead, you will be saved. For it is by believing in your heart that you are made right with God, and it is by confessing with your mouth that you are saved. (Romans 10:8-10 NLT)

Your faith in God's Word is expressed with your heart (believe) and with your mouth (confess). If you truly believe in your heart that God raised Jesus from the dead, there is no reason you should not be willing to confess Him as Lord. The moment you believe in your heart upon Jesus and confess Him as your Lord and Savior, you are born again.

It is God's ability, and our willingness and having faith that we receive this born again experience. It is not obtained by our own work as many have taught concerning earning your way into heaven. It has to come through God's power and His grace. We are unable to accomplish these things by our own work. *For it is by free grace (God's unmerited favor) that you are saved (delivered from judgment and made partakers of Christ's salvation) through [your] faith. And this [salvation] is not of yourselves [of your own doing, it came not through your own striving], but it is the gift of God; Not because of works [not the fulfillment of the Law's demands], lest any man should boast. [It is not the result of what anyone can possibly do, so no one can pride himself in it or take glory to himself.] (Ephesians 2:8-9 AMP)*

We could have never been saved had it not been for the grace of God. Man is certainly undeserving according to his own merits. It is God's power working through what Jesus has done on the cross and by His Spirit that brings about the new birth. Yet without an attitude of repentance and faith, God's power will not work in a man's heart. Man's will must be obedient to God's will before he can receive God's blessings.

When we are born again, we become brand new people on the inside. The Holy Spirit gives us New Life, where we are no longer the same. We are recreated living in union with Christ.

This means that anyone who belongs to Christ has become a new person. The old life is gone; a new life has begun! (II Corinthians 5:17 NLT)

The new birth makes you a brand new person. You are created after the image of Jesus Christ and now our actions must be evident within our life decisions. This means that within your heart, you are made to be like Christ.

Put on your new nature, and be renewed as you learn to know your Creator and become like him. (Colossians 3:10 NLT)

We must feed our minds with the Word of God so that we are renewed in our thinking, as well as continuing learning more about Jesus Christ. We accomplish this by doing what the Word of God teaches us.

Do not be conformed to this world (this age), [fashioned after and adapted to its external, superficial customs], but be transformed (changed) by the [entire] renewal of your mind [by its new ideals and its new attitude], so that you may prove [for yourselves] what is the good and acceptable and perfect will of God, even the thing which is good and acceptable and perfect [in His sight for you]. (Romans 12:2 AMP)

Coming into the Kingdom of God is what we get to enjoy.

"Giving thanks to the Father, who has qualified you to share in the inheritance of the saints in the kingdom of light. For he has rescued us from the dominion of darkness and brought us into the kingdom of the Son he loves, in whom we have redemption, the forgiveness of sins." (Colossians 1:12-14 NIV)

When you are born again, you are taken out of Satan's kingdom of darkness and you are placed into the Kingdom of Jesus, the kingdom of light. It is not something you just hope or wish for, it is a fact. The child of God does not have to be lorded over by Satan ever again. This freedom is experienced through us accepting this revelation that we no longer have to let Satan have power over us.

This new kingdom is a spiritual kingdom. However, just because salvation is basically a spiritual rebirth, does not mean that it has no effect on your body, mind, or every day living. It can and should have a great impact on every part of your life. One should experience a true change in life that will cause us to move in the right direction.

In life, there are natural laws. For example: gravity, sun, rain, plants growing, and animals reproducing, each one producing the thing it was created to do. It is the same with spiritual laws. These spiritual laws have two sides, one known as the kingdom of darkness where Satan and his cohorts operate, and the Kingdom of God His Spirit, where His angels operate. Both of these kingdoms are warring against each other. However, based on what the Word of God says, the Kingdom of God comes out victorious and can be experienced through what Jesus Christ has finished *(refer to I Corinthians 15:50-57).* When one is born again, they move from the law of sin and death to the law of the spirit of life in Christ Jesus.

For the law of the Spirit of life [which is] in Christ Jesus [the law of our new being] has freed me from the law of sin and of death. (Romans 8:2 AMP)

What we find in the law of the spirit of life is total life prosperity, which includes having wholeness in every area of your life. This would include in your spirit, soul, health, family, and finances. You must enforce this into Your New Life! You must also receive the Word of God, you must change your attitude and actions toward prosperity, know God wants to bless and prosper you, and know He is a giver and willing to give you all that He has promised in His Word. His Word is true and unchanging.

The day you accepted Jesus as your Lord and Savior, you were forgiven of all your sins; in fact, all was paid for you when He became a ransom for you. However, you do not experience that forgiveness until you receive it by faith. This can be a challenge for many people because of the many horrible things that they have done before coming to Jesus Christ. I, too, had a difficult time with this at first because I came out of a lifestyle that included being addicted to drugs and alcohol, stealing, cheating, and even spending time in jail. However, once I discovered that I had to receive forgiveness by faith, it set me free, allowing me to move onto my calling.

Even though a person may have committed many sins, they don't have to allow unbelief to keep them from receiving forgiveness.

About sin, because they do not believe in Me [trust in, rely on, and adhere to Me]. (John 16:9 AMP) Begin to trust in and rely on God, and accept that your sins are forgiven. The blood of Christ cleanses the heart the moment a person believes and confesses Him as Savior. Break the power of sin by having faith that the blood of Jesus has cleansed you from sin.

But if we are living in the light of God's presence, just as Christ is, then we have fellowship with each other, and the blood of Jesus, his Son, cleanses us from every sin. (I John 1:7 NLT)

We cannot avoid the importance of Water baptism. Though we understand that it in itself does not save, it is a very important part of the born again experience. In the Great Commission, Jesus told His disciples, ***Therefore, go and make disciples of all the nations, baptizing them in the name of the Father and the Son and the Holy Spirit. (Matthew 28:19 NLT)*** In the Jordan River, John baptized Jesus Himself.

Then Jesus went from Galilee to the Jordan River to be baptized by John. But John tried to talk him out of it. "I am the one who needs to be baptized by you," he said, "so why are you coming to me?" But Jesus said, "It should be done, for we must carry out all that God requires." So John agreed to baptize him. After his baptism, as Jesus came up out of the water, the heavens were opened and he saw the Spirit of God descending like a dove and settling on him. And a voice from heaven said, "This is my dearly loved Son, who brings me great joy." (Matthew 3:13-17 NLT)

We find this practice continued after Jesus' death, burial, resurrection, and Him ascending to the right hand of the Father. In the book of Acts, we see Peter teaching them the steps to being born again, which included Water baptism. *Peter replied, "Each of you must repent of your sins and turn to God, and be baptized in the name of Jesus Christ for the forgiveness of your sins. Then you will receive the gift of the Holy Spirit. This promise is to you, and to your children, and even to the Gentiles – all who have been called by the Lord our God." Then Peter continued preaching for a long time, strongly urging all his listeners, "Save yourselves from this crooked generation!" Those who believed what Peter said were baptized and added to the church that day - about 3,000 in all. (Acts 2:38-41 NLT)*

Water Baptism was continued by the Apostles, even the Apostle Paul was baptized after his conversion. *Instantly something like scales fell from Saul's eyes, (added by the author: his name was changed to Paul) and he regained his sight. Then he got up and was baptized. (Acts 9:18 NLT)*

He later baptized the believers at Ephesus **Acts 19:5.** Those at Cornelius' house were baptized after they had received the Holy Ghost **Acts 10:44-48**. The Philippian jailer and all his household were baptized after they had believed in Jesus **Acts 16:31-33.**

The Spirit Himself [thus] testifies together with our own spirit, [assuring us] that we are children of God. (Romans 8:16 AMP) In the *New Living Translation,* it says it like this: *For his Spirit joins with our spirit to affirm that we are God's children.*

We can have the assurance because of the Holy Spirit that lives in us removing any doubt that we are born again. This is not depended on any feelings, but only by trusting and having faith in what the Word of God says.

I have written this to you who believe in the name of the Son of God, so that you may know you have eternal life. (I John 5:13 NLT) If you meet the conditions given in God's Word for salvation, you can know you are saved. God's Word says that you can know. That is what you must stand on - His Word - not your feelings.

Pray this prayer. I want to personally invite you to call upon God, by faith, to save you. Ask Him to save you and believe that He will do it. Do not hesitate. The Scripture urges us, *"Seek ye the Lord while He may be found, call ye upon Him while He is near." (Isaiah 55:6)* **Dear Lord, I acknowledge that I am a sinner. I believe Jesus died for my sins on the cross and rose again the third day. I repent of my sins. By faith, I receive the Lord Jesus as my Savior. You promised to save me, and I believe You because You are God and cannot lie. I believe right now that the Lord Jesus is my personal Savior, and that all my sins are forgiven through His precious blood. I thank You, dear Lord, for saving me. In Jesus' Name. Amen.**

Chapter 5

Understanding Faith

Hebrews Chapter 11 is what is known as the Hall of Faith chapter of the Bible. It is where we find many of the great acts and demonstration of faith by those in the Bible. As you read this entire chapter in Hebrews 11, focus in on the lives of the men who walked in faith.

Through the act of faith is how we are born again. The Word of God tells us, ***For it is by free grace (God's unmerited favor) that you are saved (delivered from judgment and made partakers of Christ's salvation) <u>THROUGH [YOUR] FAITH</u>. And this [salvation] is not of yourselves [of your own doing, it came not through your own striving], but it is the gift of God. (Ephesians 2:8 AMP)***

We can see that the gift of eternal life is obtained through our faith. It is important for us to understand the role that faith has when coming into a relationship with Jesus. It is something that is an important part of living for Him, once being born again. A lifestyle of faith must be established and learned. This is what we want to discuss in this chapter.

What is faith? Faith is the confidence that what we hope for will actually happen; it gives us assurance about things we cannot see. (Hebrews 11:1 NLT) Now let us look at another version of the same verse. *NOW FAITH is the assurance (the confirmation, the title deed) of the things [we] hope for, being the proof of things [we] do not see and the conviction of their reality [faith perceiving as real fact what is not revealed to the senses].(Hebrews 11:1 AMP)*

Faith is in the present tense. It believes NOW. It receives NOW. It acts NOW. One of the great differences between faith and hope is in the tense. Hope is usually concerned with the future, whereas faith is most often concerned with the present.

The type of faith defined in Hebrews 11:1 is that true faith in God has assurance. When a person steps out in this type of faith, they will be standing on a solid rock. The assurance is the title deed to eternal life. We have this confident assurance that we have God's promises that He will do what He says in His Word.

Faith connects you to God; it is your admission that you are dependent upon Him and that your hope is in Him. It pleases Him because it is He you are trusting and no one and nothing else. Even though He cannot be seen, we are born again by us putting our faith in Jesus Christ and experience the change in our life. Faith is where you please God, admit your dependence upon Him, and continually seek to rely upon Him and His grace. Ask yourself these questions that only you can answer. *What has faith changed in your life? What are faith's evidences in your life? Is faith growing in your life?*

Although there may be no physical evidence for your faith, you do have sufficient evidence in God's Word. Your evidence for what you believe is your faith in God's Word. God is a witness. He will never lie. If you take God at His Word, that Word will stand good in the trial.

The best way to get faith is to hear the Word of God. It is important for you not only to hear it with your ears, but also with your heart. To hear God's Word in your heart requires openness and hunger for God's message. *So faith comes from hearing, that is, hearing the Good News about Christ. (Romans 10:17 NLT)*

Begin by speaking the Word of God aloud and allow it to become alive in you. Our faith is stimulated when we hear it. By faith, believe, receive, and confess it every day. Faith will grow as you are continually hearing God's Word.

In the Word of God, we can see that God has given everyone the exact amount of faith needed to live in this life. God has not given one person more faith and less to another. In *Acts 10:34,* **we read,** *Then Peter opened his mouth, and said, Of a truth I perceive that God is no respecter of persons.* God does not favor one over the other. Everything that God has made available has been made available to all equally. It just seems as if some have more faith than others do because they have discovered how it works and have accepted it.

For I say, through the grace given unto me, to every man that is among you, not to think of himself more highly than he ought to think; BUT TO THINK SOBERLY, ACCORDING AS GOD HATH DEALT TO EVERY MAN THE MEASURE OF FAITH. (Romans 12:3)

Paul is writing to the Christians in Rome. God has dealt to every Christian the measure of faith. However, you also have to have faith to be saved before you are a Christian. ***Romans 10:13 says, For whosoever shall call upon the name of the Lord shall be saved.*** Evidently, any person who hears God's Word and will act on it can exercise faith. That includes all who hear and obey God's Word whether saved or in the process of being saved.

People who do not hear God's Word or will not obey it do not have the God kind of faith. Faith requires hearing and obeying.

God's Word is what we need to act on. God gives us promises in His Word that provided for our every need in life. He promises a full, abundant supply. It is all yours for the asking. God just wants you to believe His Word and take what has been set before you. Here are some examples as to how we can activate our faith using God's Word concerning His favor:

Because the favor of God shields me, no sickness or disease has a right to live in my body. (Deuteronomy 7:15; Psalm 5:12)

Wealth and riches are in my house because I am empowered with His anointing and favor to draw wealth. (Deuteronomy 8:18; Psalm 112:3)

Jesus is the Apostle and High Priest over my profession, and what I profess is the Word of God concerning favor over my life. (Hebrews 3:1)

The Lord helps me to guard the door of my mouth and trains me not to speak against His favor at work in my life. (Psalm 141:3, AMP)

What you receive from Him will come as a result of your actively reaching out and claiming His promises.

"What do you want me to do for you?" Jesus asked. "My rabbi," the blind man said, "I want to see!" And Jesus said to him, "Go, for your faith has healed you." Instantly the man could see, and he followed Jesus down the road. (Mark 10:51-52 NLT)

Sometimes, people base their spiritual experiences on feelings and emotions. Problems arise when the feelings and emotions change if they have not been grounded in the Word of God. Feelings alone can bring doubt that will raise questions to whether or not the experience was genuine.

For faith to be consistent, it must be based on something with more stability than your feelings.

You are not saved because you feel saved. You are saved because you have put your faith in God's Word and acted on it. Feelings and emotions are subject to change and when it comes to faith, it cannot be based on how we feel. We live our lives on what the Word of God says, regardless of how we feel. The unchanging Word of God is what we stand on in faith.

Jesus Christ is the same yesterday, today, and forever. (Hebrews 13:8 NLT)

Feelings are influenced by what you see, what you read, and what you hear. Everyone is exposed to things that are not consistent with God's Word. If these things control your feelings and your feelings control your faith, you can be a Christian controlled by changing circumstances ruled by emotions and feelings.

Your faith must be controlled by God's Word, not by what you feel, not by what circumstances look like, and not by what others tell you. ***For we walk by faith [we regulate our lives and conduct ourselves by our conviction or*** *belief respecting man's relationship to God and divine things, with trust and holy fervor; thus we walk] not by sight or appearance. (II Corinthians 5:7 AMP)*

So we don't look at the troubles we can see now; rather, we fix our gaze on things that cannot be seen. For the things we see now will soon be gone, but the things we cannot see will last forever. (II Corinthians 4:18 NLT)

God's Word is eternal and will never pass away. Your spiritual eyes must be focused on God by looking at His Word.

Your New Life

Chapter 6

Healing Is Yours

If you are a believer, you have already experienced life changes by being born again. When being saved, God did not leave anything out. Everything including healing has been made available to you. Just as sickness came through Adam's sin, healing came when Jesus paid the price for that sin.

If you will listen carefully to the voice of the Lord your God and do what is right in his sight, obeying his commands and keeping all his decrees, then I will not make you suffer any of the diseases I sent on the Egyptians; for I am the <u>LORD WHO HEALS YOU</u>. (Exodus 15:26 NLT)

God promises that if the people obey Him, they would be free from diseases that plagued the Egyptians. We have to believe that God is speaking these words to us right now. We must be willing to accept the message that it is God's will for you to be healed and that He has opened the door for His divine health.

He forgives all my sins and heals all my diseases. He ransoms me from death and surrounds me with love and tender mercies. (Psalm 103:2-3 NLT)

Notice that forgiveness is one of God's benefits. When Jesus Christ was on the cross of Calvary, He not only died for our sins; He did more than that. What this means is that Jesus included everything in our lives that falls short of the glory and the perfection of God's original plan. *For all have sinned, and come short of the glory of God. (Romans 3:23)* God is concerned about both your spiritual healing and your physical healing.

The prophet Isaiah wrote about God's suffering servant, the Messiah or Redeemer of Israel. He was writing about Jesus taking your punishment for your sins. Jesus suffered for you in every way you deserved to suffer: physically, mentally, and spiritually. He did it in order that you might not have to suffer these things. He was your substitute, your Savior.

Yet it was our weaknesses he carried; it was our sorrows that weighed him down. And we thought his troubles were a punishment from God, a punishment for his own sins! But he was pierced for our rebellion, crushed for our sins.

He was beaten so we could be whole. He was whipped so we could be healed. All of us, like sheep, have strayed away. We have left God's paths to follow our own. Yet the LORD laid on him the sins of us all. (Isaiah 53:4-6 NLT)

The prophet Isaiah wrote about Jesus who would take our sicknesses and pains. In the *New Testament,* we see this *Old Testament* fulfillment. **This fulfilled the word of the Lord through the prophet Isaiah, who said, "He took our sicknesses and removed our diseases. (Matthew 8:17 NLT)** Jesus suffered as He took your place and God's judgment, for sin fell on Him.

While Jesus walked the face of the earth, He ministered healing to every part of man's spirit, soul, and body. He cast out devils, healed the sick, forgave sins, and restored wholeness to those tormented by Satan. In recording these events, Matthew quoted from Isaiah, *Yet it was our weaknesses he carried; it was our sorrows that weighed him down. And we thought his troubles were a punishment from God, a punishment for his own sins! (Isaiah 53:4 NLT)*

Not only did He take your diseases and all of your sicknesses on the cross, but also during His ministry, He healed many that were sick. He did this in relation to sins also. Not only did He take your sins on the cross, but He also forgave men of their sins before the crucifixion. This is an amazing revelation that before we were born, He provided a way for all to have an opportunity to be restored from a broken relationship between God and man.

Peter was a man who witnessed the mock trial of Jesus. He was well acquainted with the happenings on Calvary. He wrote about the affects that Jesus' suffering would have on your life. He mentions both the spiritual and the physical results of Christ's atonement.

Who his own self bare our sins in his own body on the tree, that we, being dead to sins, should live unto righteousness: BY WHOSE STRIPES YE WERE HEALED. (I Peter 2:24)

The phrase "by whose stripes you were healed" is a direct reference to *Isaiah 53:5 But he was wounded for our transgressions, he was bruised for our iniquities: the chastisement of our peace was upon him, AND WITH HIS STRIPES WE ARE HEALED.* We can see in *MARK 15:15 Jesus, when he had scourged him, to be crucified.* The physical punishment that He took was for your healing.

All the punishment Jesus received before and during the crucifixion was for your healing - spirit, soul, and body.

Before Adam's sin in the garden, there was no sin or death on earth. After his disobedience, sin and death with all of their evil companions (hatred, bitterness, jealousy, sickness, disease, and torment) entered the world. *Wherefore, as by one man sin entered into the world, and death by sin; and so death passed upon all men, for that all have sinned. (Romans 5:12)*

Jesus was sent to re-establish and restore what man had before the fall. He was the Redeemer, the one sent to buy you back from the dominion of Satan. Jesus loosed the people who were captive to Satan's devices. He healed the sick, delivered the oppressed, opened prison doors, and preached the good news.

This Scripture, as well as all four Gospels, clearly reveals that the devil oppresses people with sickness, and Jesus heals people who are sick. Never confuse these two. God desires an abundant life for you, and the devil wants to steal, to kill, and to destroy. *The thief comes only in order to steal and kill and destroy. I came that they may have and enjoy life, and have it in abundance (to the full, till it overflows). (John 10:10 AMP)*

God is interested in your health spiritually and physically. He wants your body to be just as free from Satan's influence as He does your heart.

Beloved, I wish above all things that thou mayest prosper and be in health, even as thy soul prospereth. (III John 2)

Not only are you to live holy and pure lives in your body, but it is also possible for you to live in health. You have been bought with the blood of Christ. The price has been paid for spiritual and physical health. *You were bought with a price [purchased with a preciousness and paid for, made His own]. So then, honor God and bring glory to Him in your body. (I Corinthians 6:20 AMP)*

There was a curse pronounced upon those who would not keep God's laws *(Deuteronomy 28:15-68)*. This curse generally included poverty, sickness, and death. Since all men were sinners, there was no man who could fully keep all God's laws *(Romans 3:23)*. Jesus entered the earth as a man and lived His life without sin. As He hung on the cross, He was actually made to be a curse for you as your substitute. He took the curse you deserved. He took your poverty, your sickness, and your death (sin), so that you might receive the blessings God had promised to Abraham and those keeping his law. These include an abundant supply for every need in your life ***(Deuteronomy 28:1-14). Jesus Christ (the Messiah) is [always] the same, yesterday, today, [yes] and forever (to the ages). (Hebrews 13:8 AMP)*** Jesus was moved by love and compassion for all of humanity. Jesus continues to this day to bring healing and to meet the needs of all people. He is still the same. His compassion has not stopped. He loves you just as much as He did those in the time of His earthly ministry. His power is not stopped just because He is no longer visibly in our midst. His power and effectiveness are even greater today because He can be present in all places at all times by His Spirit. We know from the book of Acts that the healing ministry of Christ did not stop with His death and resurrection. It continued through the twelve disciples and the other believers. ***And then he told them, "Go into all the world and preach the Good News to everyone. Anyone who believes and is baptized will be saved. But anyone who refuses to believe will be condemned. These miraculous signs will accompany those who believe: They will cast out demons in my name, and they will speak in*** *new languages. They will be able to handle snakes with safety, and if they drink anything poisonous, it won't hurt them. They will be able to place their hands on the sick, and they will be healed." When the Lord Jesus had finished talking with them, he was taken up into heaven and sat down in the place of honor at God's right hand. (Acts 16:15-19 NLT)*

People received healing under Jesus' ministry in numerous ways. Today, men can continue to receive healing.

One particularly important method is anointing with oil and praying the prayer of faith. It demonstrates to us that God's power can be ministered by believers and thus shows that healing did not end when Christ died or when the apostles died. Healing is still provided for you today. *Are any of you sick? You should call for the elders of the church to come and pray over you, anointing you with oil in the name of the Lord. Such a prayer offered in faith will heal the sick, and the Lord will make you well. And if you have committed any sins, you will be forgiven. (James 5:14-15 NLT)*

Your New Life

Chapter 7

Baptism in the Holy Spirit

It is revealed and shown through different events how the Holy Spirit Baptism expressed Himself to mankind. It is revealed to the believer that Jesus will baptize them with the Holy Spirit and with fire. *I indeed baptize you with water unto repentance, but he that cometh after me is mightier than I, whose shoes I am not worthy to bear: he shall baptize you with the Holy Ghost, and with fire. (Matthew 3:11). For John truly baptized with water; but ye shall be baptized with the Holy Ghost not many days hence. (Acts 1:5)*

Jesus spoke to the apostles just before He ascended back into heaven, and in one of these meetings, he was eating a meal with them, and said, *"Do not leave Jerusalem until the Father sends you the gift he promised, as I told you before. John baptized with water, but in just a few days, you will be baptized with the Holy Spirit." (Acts 1:4-5 NLT)*

When Does it All Begin

The moment a person becomes a Christian, they receive the Holy Spirit. Regeneration takes place, or new birth, which is an inner recreating of the fallen human nature. This is a gracious sovereign action of the Holy Spirit. Every Believer has the Holy Spirit. *Jesus answered, "Truly, truly, I say to you, unless one is born of water and the Spirit he cannot enter into the kingdom of God. That which is born of the flesh is flesh, and that which is born of the Spirit is spirit. "Do not be amazed that I said to you, 'You must be born again.' "The wind blows where it wishes and you hear the sound of it, but do not know where it comes from and where it is going ; so is everyone who is born of the Spirit." (John 3:5-8 NASB)*

The Holy Spirit comes to dwell in every person who puts his or her trust in Christ Jesus for salvation. The Holy Spirit is God's very life that He breathes into us producing a new life in Christ.

And when He had said this, He breathed on them and said to them, "Receive the Holy Spirit." (John 20:22 NASB)

The assignment of the Holy Spirit is to convict every one of us of sin and draw the heart of the sinner to Christ, bringing them into right standing through the New Birth. *"And He, when He comes, will convict the world concerning sin and righteousness and judgment; concerning sin, because they do not believe in Me; and concerning righteousness, because I go to the Father and you no longer see Me; and concerning judgment, because the ruler of this world has been judged." (John 16:8-11 NASB.)*

However, God has more for you. In addition to blessing you, He wants to use you to bless others.

Outpouring of the Holy Spirit

The Spirit came, as foretold by John and Jesus, **(Acts 1:4-5; Luke 24:49***).* The Spirit came and was accompanied by audible and visual signs. The sound was like that of a mighty rushing wind **(Acts 2:2***).* Divided tongues were as of fire sitting upon each of them **(Acts 2:3).** The Spirit filled or baptized them **(Acts 2:4).** Every man heard them speak in his own language **(Acts 2:6).** Those who spoke were "Galileans" **(***Acts 2:7***)**, suggesting it was the apostles. The significance here is that the apostles were from Galilee and the 120 disciples were from all over Palestine. Here, we see the manifestation of the Spirit, by the believers, speaking as the Spirit moved in them. The reaction of the crowd was mixed. They were amazed and in doubt, wondering as they were talking to each other saying, what can this mean? Some were amazed and perplexed, while others mocked, accusing the apostles of being drunk **(Acts 2:12-13).**

The Promise of the Father

After the resurrection, Jesus told his disciples, *"And, behold, I send the promise of my Father upon you: but tarry ye in the city of Jerusalem, until ye be endued with power from on high." (Luke 24:49)*

The baptism of the Holy Spirit was called the promise of the Father in this passage. Jesus said they would be endued with power from on high. These followers would be endowed with God's power to be witnesses of Jesus. According to His instruction, some 120 followers of Jesus, including the disciples, met together to wait for the promise of the Father.

When the Day of Pentecost had fully come, they were all with one accord in one place. And suddenly there came a sound from heaven, as of a rushing mighty wind, and it filled the whole house where they were sitting. Then there appeared to them divided tongues, as of fire, and one sat upon each of them. And they were all filled with the Holy Spirit and began to speak with other tongues, as the Spirit gave them utterance. (Acts 2:1-4 NKJV)

Empowered to Witness

They would see the expression of the Holy Spirit come upon them. The word "upon" could give the meaning of overtake, to come, arrive, descending, and operating in one. This shows that the Holy Spirit came to them to empower them to do the things that every believer was commissioned to do and that was and is to be a witness. *But ye shall receive power, after that the Holy Ghost is come upon you: and ye shall be witnesses unto me both in Jerusalem, and in all Judaea, and in Samaria, and unto the uttermost part of the earth. (Acts 1:8)*

An important reason for the baptism of the Holy Spirit is power for witnessing of the living Christ. It could be termed enablement or ability from God.

The baptism in the Holy Spirit is a promised blessing that was spoken of by the Prophet Joel. It was a blessing that was poured out upon all mankind for the purpose of fulfilling the plans and purposes of mankind. God has always made available, to all believers, a way for them to be used and to make a difference in the Kingdom of God. It was never His purpose to do all of these things by Himself. He has given us His power and His wisdom and His ability to bring hope and peace to this world. We are to bring the end time harvest, but this is what was spoken of through the prophet Joel. *"And it shall be in the last days;"* God says, *"That I will pour forth of my spirit on all mankind; and your sons and your daughters shall prophesy, and your young men shall see visions, and your old men shall dream dreams." (Acts 2:16-17 NASB) "For the promise is for you and your children and for all who are far off, as many as the Lord our God will call to Himself." (Acts 2:39 NASB)*

Out of His Heart Flows Rivers of Living Water

Jesus described the Holy Spirit as rivers of living water that would flow out of the believer's innermost being. *On the last day, that great day of the feast, Jesus stood and cried out, saying, "If anyone thirsts, let him come to Me and drink. He who believes in Me, as the Scripture has said, out of his heart will flow rivers of living water." But this He spoke concerning the Spirit, whom those believing in Him would receive; for the Holy Spirit was not yet given, because Jesus was not yet glorified. (John 7:37-39 NKJV)*

The Holy Spirit produces rivers of life, love, joy, peace, and power to flow out of your spirit to meet the needs of others. Jesus said those that believe upon Him SHOULD RECEIVE THE HOLY SPIRIT.

The Comforter and Teacher

Jesus taught His disciples concerning the ministry of the Holy Spirit in their lives. One of the names He used in speaking of the Holy Spirit was Comforter. He also said the Holy Spirit would teach and guide the believers.

And I will pray the Father, and He will give you another Helper, that He may abide with you forever - the Spirit of truth, whom the world cannot receive, because it neither sees Him nor knows Him; but you know Him, for He dwells with you and will be in you. (John 14:16-17 NKJV)

Although Jesus and the Father and the Holy Spirit are One, Jesus prayed to the Father and the Father gave the Holy Spirit through Jesus.

An unbeliever cannot receive the Holy Spirit, for Jesus said the world cannot receive Him. The Holy Spirit can only come upon someone who accepts Jesus as his or her Savior. *"the Spirit of truth, whom the world cannot receive, because it neither sees Him nor knows Him; but you know Him, for He dwells with you and will be in you. (John 14:17 NKJV)*

It is important to read the Word of God for this is the Truth. The Holy Spirit at the time of need brings to your remembrance the words of Jesus. He also teaches you how to apply God's Word in your life. *"But when the Helper comes, whom I shall send to you from the Father, the Spirit of truth who proceeds from the Father, He will testify of Me." (John 15:26 NKJV)*

The ministry of the Holy Spirit is to testify of Jesus to the believer. He is the witness in us *(Romans 8:16).* He opens your eyes to what is promised to you in Christ.

However, when He, the Spirit of truth, has come, He will guide you into all truth; for He will not speak on His own authority, but whatever He hears He will speak; and He will tell you things to come. He will glorify Me, for He will take of what is Mine and declare it to you. (John 16:13-14 NKJV)

The truth is in God's Word. The Holy Spirit guides you into an understanding of the truth as revealed in the Scriptures. What He hears from God, He speaks to you. He will always glorify Jesus and be consistent with the Word of God.

God's will is for every believer to be filled with His Spirit. His desire is that you be continually overflowing with His Spirit. Remember, Jesus COMMANDED the disciples not to leave Jerusalem until they had been endued with power *(Luke 24:49), (Acts 1:4)*. He also said those who believe on Him SHOULD receive the Holy Spirit *(John 7:39)*.

Ask and You Shall Receive

Knowing that it is God's will for you to be filled with the Holy Spirit gives you confidence by asking Him to baptize you with the Holy Spirit.

And this is the confidence (the assurance, the privilege of boldness) which we have in Him: [we are sure] that if we ask anything (make any request) according to His will (in agreement with His own plan), He listens to and hears us. And if (since) we [positively] know that He listens to us in whatever we ask, we also know [with settled and absolute knowledge] that we have [granted us as our present possessions] the requests made of Him. (I John 5:14-15 AMP)

When we know what God's will is, there should not be any problem having confidence in Him responding to our request because we know He hears us. God responds to His will and the Word of God is His will. The promise of the Holy Spirit is His will, so ask and you shall receive.

Speaking in Tongues

These signs will accompany those who have believed: in My name they will cast out demons, they will speak with new tongues. (Mark 16:17 NASB) Jesus called these things signs. These signs therefore confirm the ministries of Christ's disciples - casting out demons and speaking in tongues.

Again, we see Paul calling tongues a sign. *So then tongues are for a sign, not to those who believe but to unbelievers; but prophecy is for a sign, not to unbelievers but to those who believe. (I Corinthians 14:22 NASB)*

Not only did we see the sign of the sound of wind and the sign of fire that sat upon each one, we also saw the sign of speech in tongues in Acts 2.

When it comes to speaking in tongues, it is a sign of someone that has been baptized with the Holy Spirit, and as a sign of God's presence in a believer's life.

The 120 believers (Jews) all spoke with other tongues on the day of Pentecost when they received the baptism of the Holy Spirit *(Acts 2:4)*. The Gentiles in the house of Cornelius spoke with tongues when the Holy Spirit came on them *(Acts 10:44-48)*. Likewise, the people at Ephesus spoke in tongues when the Holy Spirit came on them *(Acts 19:6)*.

The Word of God gives an extensive teaching as to the purpose and use of tongues in public worship. First, it was to be a sign to the unbeliever *(I Corinthians 14:21-22)*. Second, it was used to bring edification, exhortation, and comfort to the believer *(I Corinthians 14:3-5)*.

Third, it is intended to bring the congregation to a place of prayer and praise concerning the gift of tongues *(I Corinthians 14:13-16)*. Paul encouraged those who spoke in tongues to pray for interpretation.

Gifts of the Spirit

We see the first thing Paul mentions about the gifts. *Now about the spiritual gifts (the special endowments of supernatural energy), brethren, I do not want you to be misinformed. (I Corinthians 12:1 AMP)* As we can see here, Paul wanted to make sure that the believers would not be ignorant about these gifts.

Now there are distinctive varieties and distributions of endowments (gifts, extraordinary powers distinguishing certain Christians, due to the power of divine grace operating in their souls by the Holy Spirit) and they vary, but the [Holy] Spirit remains the same. And there are distinctive varieties of service and ministration, but it is the same Lord [Who is served]. And there are distinctive varieties of operation [of working to accomplish things], but it is the same God Who inspires and energizes them all in all. But to each one is given the manifestation of the [Holy] Spirit [the evidence, the spiritual illumination of the Spirit] for good and profit. To one is given in and through the [Holy] Spirit [the power to speak] a message of wisdom, and to another [the power to express] a word of knowledge and understanding according to the same [Holy] Spirit; To another [wonder-working] faith by the same [Holy] Spirit, to another the extraordinary powers of healing by the one Spirit; To another the working of miracles, to another prophetic insight (the gift of interpreting the divine will and purpose); to another the ability to discern and distinguish between [the utterances of true] spirits [and false ones], to another various kinds of [unknown] tongues, to another the ability to interpret [such] tongues. All these [gifts, achievements, abilities] are inspired and brought to pass by one and the same [Holy] Spirit, Who apportions to each person individually [exactly] as He chooses. (I Corinthians 12:4-11 AMP)

There is a variety of gifts that the Spirit gives to believers to build up the body of Christ. Each person may at different times minister with any number of the gifts as the Spirit wills.

So we, numerous as we are, are one body in Christ (the Messiah) and individually we are parts one of another [mutually dependent on one another]. Having gifts (faculties, talents, qualities) that differ according to the grace given us, let us use them: [He whose gift is] prophecy, [let him prophesy] according to the proportion of his faith; [He whose gift is] practical service, let him give himself to serving; he who teaches, to his teaching; He who exhorts (encourages), to his exhortation; he who contributes, let him do it in simplicity and liberality; he who gives aid and superintends, with zeal and singleness of mind; he who does acts of mercy, with genuine cheerfulness and joyful eagerness. (Romans 12:5-8 AMP)

The operation of these gifts will only take place as God wills, not necessarily when we want. For God is the only one who ultimately knows what and when things are needed. The purpose of the supernatural gifts is to offer individuals, who have these gifts; to operate in God's all knowing power. When God gives these gifts, He holds us responsible when He releases us to be used in them. When we operate in these gifts, it is vital to self-examine our motives and secure the Fruit of the Spirit is in operation in our life, otherwise, we would be operating in these gifts in vain. These gifts are supernatural; they were given to bring edification always and with the purpose to bring help.

Your New Life

Chapter 8

The Abundant Life

God has made provisions for every Christian to live in victory and abundance. Just because others may not be experiencing victory in their lives does not mean that God has not provided it. He has done everything in His power to give His children the authority and provisions needed to live triumphantly on this earth.

God wants His people to enjoy life in abundance, to the full, until it overflows. This is fulfilling the will of God. When you focus on the Word of God, you will begin to experience the abundant life.

Since becoming a Believer, you have been given authority here on earth. Never forget that Satan's purpose is to steal, kill, and destroy. ***Then Jesus said to them again, "Most assuredly, I say to you, I am the door of the sheep. All who ever came before Me are thieves and robbers, but the sheep did not hear them. I am the door. If anyone enters by Me, he will be saved, and will go in and out and*** *find pasture. The thief does not come except to steal, and to kill, and to destroy. I have come that they may have life, and that they may have it more abundantly. (John 10:7-10 NKJV)*

We must guard ourselves from the enemy and do not give him authority over things in your life. When coming to Christ, you have been given authority over the enemy. There is no need to tolerate sin in your life because we already know that Jesus came so that we may have life and have it more abundantly.

We must guard our mouth from saying things that are contrary to the Word of God. Death and life are in the power of the tongue, and they who indulge in it shall eat the fruit of it [for death or life] *(Proverbs 18:21 AMP).* If we are not careful with our words, we risk saying things that empower the devil. Rather, speak life-giving words. *Jesus came so that you might have and enjoy life in abundance, to the full, until it overflows (John 10:10 AMP).*

The Greek translation of the word "life" is Zoë, which means, "absolute fullness of life; the life of God." Jesus wants you to live in the fullness of life. Your life should overflow to the point that not only are your needs met, but others as well. If you are not enjoying life, you are not fulfilling the will of God for your life. Abundance applies to every area of life—relationships, health, finances, etc. Real prosperity is having everything you need to do for what God has called you to do.

I heard *Creflo Dollar teach on steps to abundance. He says,* You must have the Word of God. The Word of God determines your thinking. Your thinking will determine your emotions. Your emotions will determine your decisions. Your decisions will determine your actions. Your actions will determine your habits. Your habits will determine your character. Then you will arrive at your destination, which are abundance, prosperity, and overflow.

As you can see, it starts with the Word of God and as you release it, it begins to have a domino effect resulting in true success in every area of your life.

The Word of God, when attended to each day, will lead to success and blessings. ***This Book of the Law shall not depart out of your mouth, but you shall meditate on it day and night, that you may observe and do according to all that is written in it. FOR THEN YOU SHALL MAKE***

YOUR WAY PROSPEROUS, AND THEN YOU SHALL DEAL WISELY AND HAVE GOOD SUCCESS. (Joshua 1:8 AMP)

Keeping Your Heart Right

To enjoy the abundant life and continued overflow of God's goodness in our lives, we must make sure our motives, attitudes, and thoughts originate in the heart. Many times, Christians focus on outward manifestations of their faith, but God is concerned with the purity of a person's heart. It does not impress God if we look good on the outside; God wants us to be good all the time. He knows what is in our heart and what we really think. The condition of your heart determines the outcome of your life. Believers must judge their hearts to make sure their motives are pure.

When our heart is not right, it prevents us from receiving all that God has for our lives. The releasing of God's blessings oftentimes depends on a right heart. *Who may climb the mountain of the LORD? Who may stand in his holy place? Only those whose hands and hearts are pure, who do not worship idols and never tell lies. They*

will receive the LORD's blessing and have a right relationship with God their savior. (Psalm 24:3-5 NLT)

Many people do good things and even have many luxuries, but the Bible says that only the people with clean hands and pure hearts will succeed. If we truly love God and want to please God, we should on a regular basis judge our own hearts to make sure our motives are pure. Many people think that just because a person does many nice things, that they have a good heart. I have seen people and I personally have done many nice things that looked good from the outside, but on the inside, the heart certainly was not right or done with right motives and attitude.

To be able to have every area experience overflowing, one must continue to ensure a pure heart.

God blesses those whose hearts are pure, for they will see God. (Matthew 5:8 NLT)

When we maintain a pure heart, God's blessings manifest whenever we need them. Some people try to please men, but being a fake Christian does not please God. Our actions may look good and people may be impressed, but God looks in our hearts.

As believers, we must keep our hearts pure and holy in the presence of the Lord. Holiness is an inward agreement with God that manifests as an outward change.

Believers should never cover their faults or pretend that they do not exist. Instead, they should confess their faults to trustworthy people who will pray for their healing and restoration. *Confess to one another therefore your faults (your slips, your false steps, your offenses, your sins) and pray [also] for one another, that you may be healed and restored [to a spiritual tone of mind and heart]. The earnest (heartfelt, continued) prayer of a righteous man makes tremendous power available [dynamic in its working]. (James 5:16 AMP)*

Do not be a pretender, be real with a real desire to what is right. Look what Jesus said. *Woe to you, scribes and Pharisees, pretenders (hypocrites)! For you are like tombs that have been whitewashed, which look beautiful on the outside but inside are full of dead men's bones and everything impure. (Matthew 23:27 AMP)*

Those who pretend to be something are more concerned with their outward appearance than the condition of their hearts. Believers who misrepresent themselves end up leading ineffective lives. The Bible says that God desires truth in the inward parts *(Psalm 51:6).*

Satan desires to contaminate Believers' hearts. If the enemy can pollute our hearts, he can control the course of our lives. Satan's goal is to get Believers to compromise, so that we will go against our convictions and enter into sin.

The Word instructs us to guard our hearts from pollution *(Proverbs 4:20-25).* We can guard our hearts when we read, meditate on, and speak aloud the Word of God daily. We can guard our hearts by being mindful of what we see, hear, and say. People who are pure at heart try to see the good in everyone *(Titus 1:15, AMP).*

Equipped for Battle

Therefore put on God's complete armor, that you may be able to resist and stand your ground on the evil day [of danger], and, having done all [the crisis demands], to stand [firmly in your place]. Stand therefore [hold your ground], having tightened the belt of truth around your loins and having put on the breastplate of integrity and of moral rectitude and right standing with God. And having shod your feet in preparation [to face the enemy with the firm-footed stability, the promptness, and the readiness produced by the good news] of the Gospel of peace. Lift up over all the [covering] shield of saving faith, upon which you can quench all the flaming missiles of the wicked [one]. And take the helmet of salvation and the sword that the Spirit wields, which is the Word of God. Pray at all times (on every occasion, in every season) in the Spirit, with all [manner of] prayer and entreaty. To that end keep alert and watch with strong purpose and perseverance, interceding in behalf of all the saints (God's consecrated people). (Ephesians 6:13-18 AMP)

There is definitely a battle to wage with the evil powers. However, God has given you all the armor needed. He has given you weapons that no power of Satan can stop. Your command is to *"put on the whole armor of God..." **(Ephesians 6:11)**.* Not even the gates of hell can stand against the fully armed church of the Lord Jesus Christ ***(Matthew 16:18)**.*

For the weapons of our warfare are not physical [weapons of flesh and blood], but they are mighty before God for the overthrow and destruction of strongholds, [Inasmuch as we] refute arguments and theories and reasonings and every proud and lofty thing that sets itself up against the [true] knowledge of God; and we lead every thought and purpose away captive into the obedience of Christ (the Messiah, the Anointed One). (II Corinthians 10:4-5 AMP)

The weapons God has provided give you the authority to pull down every fortress that Satan tries to build against you. He is powerless in the face of God's armor and weapons.

God Is Our Supplier

And my God will liberally supply (fill to the full) your every need according to His riches in glory in Christ Jesus. (Philippians 4:19 AMP)

God is your source. He supplies your need. The basis for that supply is all of the riches in glory of Christ Jesus. The supply is unlimited. As you seek first the Kingdom of God and His righteousness, all these things shall be added unto you as we can see. *But seek (aim at and strive after) first of all His kingdom and His righteousness (His way of doing and being right), and then all these things taken together will be given you besides. (Matthew 6:33 AMP)*

Continue in Every Good Work

As you give your life totally to God and His Kingdom, you know that God will gladly give you all of His life. The Christian who gives his best to God and expects God's best becomes extremely useful in the work of the Kingdom.

And God is able to make all grace (every favor and earthly blessing) come to you in abundance, so that you may always and under all circumstances and whatever the need be self-sufficient [possessing enough to require no aid or support and furnished in abundance for every good work and charitable donation]. (II Corinthians 9:8 AMP)

The most important thing to remember in living the abundant life is: Make God first and treat others with love. He will supply all the needs and make His grace abound in you, so that you will never lack in any good work to which He calls you.

About the Author

Robert J. Mullen is a Senior Pastor with an Apostolic calling to the nations. On December 14, 1991, he was supernaturally saved and delivered from a life of addiction. He received his call to preach in January 1992 while he was driving home from work one night. Robert J. Mullen accepted the call to preach and preached his first sermon in December 1992. From the beginning of his calling into ministry, his mission has been to minister to people the message of hope, and help them to see their God given potential to be successful in every area of their life. In addition, throughout his many years of ministry, he has continued to seek to do just that.

With being a Senior Pastor in Missouri, Michigan, and California, and planting one church, starting Walk on the Water Faith Ministries, a ministry geared to raising and supporting leaders nationally and internationally along with serving as a Youth Director, as well as a successful traveling ministry throughout the world, he has taken his message to thousands. Robert continues to fulfill his ministry to bring the message of hope for all people. His commitment to Christ, and remaining focused on integrity in ministry and life has made him one who is loved and respected by many.

Robert has completed his ministry studies through Messenger College and continued to pursue his AA, BA through School of Bible Theology. He has been known for bringing the Word of God with simplicity and relevance helping to bring greater understanding. Robert has proven in his own life that no matter whom you are and where you have been, God can change your heart, develop your life through His Word, and offer help to discover your destiny.

Robert met his wife Tabatha in Camdenton, Missouri while working together in a restaurant. They have been married for over 20 years and have five children and three grandchildren. Tabatha is currently serving as Co-Pastor at Word of Life Ministries, Youth Ministries, and Ladies Ministry.